Who We Are

Who We Are

Our Lives and the Human Condition

HERBERT SPOHN

iUniverse, Inc.
Bloomington

Who We Are
Our Lives and the Human Condition

iUniverse books may be ordered through booksellers or by contacting:

iUniverse
1663 Liberty Drive
Bloomington, IN 47403
www.iuniverse.com
1-800-Authors (1-800-288-4677)

ISBN: 978-1-4759-7055-5 (sc)
ISBN: 978-1-4759-7056-2 (e)

Library of Congress Control Number: 2013900492

Printed in the United States of America

iUniverse rev. date: 02/01/2013

Acknowledgements:

It is with pleasure and gratitude that I acknowledge the contributions to this book of several individuals. To begin with. my book would not have come into existence without the professional and technical contributions made by Susan Liening. Both her literary judgment as copy editor and her technical skills in the preparation of a virtually flawless text, contributed significantly to the quality of "Who We Are."

The critiques, judgments and guidance in the formulation and selection of numerous poems for inclusion in the book of Al Bernstein, Judy Nagy and Rue Cromwell contributed materially to my book.

Finally, it is of particular importance to call attention to the Cover Painting by Barbara Waterman Peters, a prominent Topeka, Kansas artist. Her stunningly beautiful rendition symbolizes the essence of "Who We Are"

Romantic Love

Falling in Love

How do I know my love?
In many ways,
I know her not.

How would I know my love?
In moments when she laughs,
in hours when I long for her.

How do I love her?
I have just begun
to find my way into her heart.

I see you
across the table
in a restaurant.

You smile,
softly,
something unspoken.

I hear you.
I know
you love me.

I am moved
beyond measure.

I sensed your gentle softness
pressing against my thigh.
Your fingertips
danced on my skin.
I breathed your air.

You touched me,
and I exulted.

All that has come and gone
has rooted me in disbelief
that I would ever trust in love
such as you have so freely given me.
You have enabled me, in turn,
to love you with all my heart,
without the burden of indebtedness.

Being in Love

You grieve the death
of the one you loved,
and when you're done,
you know a guilty truth.

Funerals can open doors
that long were closed.
Well-guarded boundaries
can now be crossed.
Ties that were broken
are readily repaired.

But on occasion,
you find a photograph
of the one you loved.
Forgotten feelings break
the surface of your life.

For a long moment
time stands still.
You are in love again
with the one you loved.
But then it's over.

All that is left
is a soft glow
that lights your way
back through a door
left open,
when your loved one died.

A dead lover
stirs in his grave.
In the hollow tongue
of the dead, he shouts:
"I loved you better
than he does now."
Only the silence hears him.

That pain is sweet
when you find rueful joy
in gain by whom you love,
that you must reckon as your loss.

Only in the mirror of your eyes
do I see my face transformed by love.
No other glass shows me such reflection.

Only love matters.
That you love me,
that I love you,
makes us whole.

There is no other comfort
but in the moment we embrace.
There is no other joy
save in each other's arms.

Our love heals wounds.
It eases pain.
We know that we must die,
but surely,
such love transcends our lives.

Romantic Love and Its Vicissitudes

We are in love
and thereby hostage
to each other's high regard.

We are at risk.
A word unspoken
may shatter self-esteem.

Perhaps tomorrow
a glance aside
will break your heart.

From long ago
another speaks.
You loved him more?

What can we do
but hold each other fast
in trusting expectation?

If you're in love,
beholden to a lover,
there is the chance you are in debt.

Attention must be paid
to her, to him.
A lapse is costly.
Injury must be allayed,
and the rift resolved
by gifts, by words, by kisses.

Giving a gift in love
entails a risk.
She may not like it.
And he may find
she has mistaken him
for who he thinks he's not.

Then if your lover catches
another lover's eye,
he/she may thus incur a debt
that cannot be repaid.

A Marriage

I love you.
What have I given you?
You love me?
What have I gained?

Are we not in a bargain?
You give me tokens,
no more than what you give
do I return.

How long does our bargain last?
When you run out of tokens?
When I begin to cheat?

I will not
I cannot
forgive you for promises denied.
Would I not grant
that I did not at any time
deserve to have your promises fulfilled?

Were I to forgive you,
it is I who would be beggared
and unworthy of anything
other than what
you've ever given me.

Upon your guilty pain,
now that I have left you,
my sense of my own worth depends.

Do not forgive me.
I have not failed you.

Do not forgive me.
You were all I desired.

Do not forgive me.
I loved you.

Do not forgive me.
You never loved me.

Do not forgive me.
I do not forgive you.

A Wife Remembered

The three individually titled poems that follow are linked in the mode of a mode of a Memoriam

A Fragment of a Marriage

"You sure tear up a bed,"
you said.

So we slept apart from each other
except on nights when we made love,
but then only for a little while.

"I don't like this modern art,
this painter Picasso.
His faces are ugly.
I like pictures of flowers
and pictures of the West.
I love those big skies,"
you said.

So we didn't go to museums.
We bought pictures of flowers
from old ladies in a painting group
and hung them in the bedroom.

"I don't know why you spend so much time with her.
I know what you're going to say:
'She's a colleague. We work together.'
But when we're at a conference, out of town,
you're always spending time with her.
I don't dislike her,
but I wouldn't want her as a friend,"
you said.

I said nothing.

A Wife Dying

Is it she,
and do I love her now,
bedfast, shrunken,
empty skin sagging from her arms,
eyes huge in her waxen face?

"Please do not leave me,"
she begs.
It is not out of love I stay,
not out of compassion.
I owe her.
I owe her more than thirty years.
It is not finished.

Asleep, she is awake.
Eyes shut,
yet open.
On guard,
eluding he who stalks her.
Her realm is continuity.
Her battlements are expectations.
From this high ground
she stares at me
and begs:
"Please stay.
I'm still alive."

In hospice I saw her.
No, I saw a shadow on a wall.
Could she have stood nearby?

Her shadow moved,
then it was gone.

In the dark now,
I heard a voice,
a word.
I wasn't sure.
Was it goodbye?

In hospice the nurses called me
to witness her death.
When her heart stopped,
I kissed her,
not in passion,
not yet in grief,
but in tribute.

A Widower's Love Song

Did I think about my wife
in the years following her death?
When my grieving was done, less and less.

Now, when a memory of her comes to mind
I feel no grief, no sorrow,
sometimes guilt for feeling nothing.

Still, one day, not long ago
I was trembling with longing for her.
I was helplessly in love again.

I saw her in a photograph
taken years ago on a cruise.
She was smiling at me, almost laughing.

I wanted to hold her again,
to kiss her again.
To have her in my life again.

My passion ebbed.
As I put the picture back in its folder,
I felt empty.

"My dear, you were young
in my life so many years.
I have not forgotten you."

Our Lives:
Experience and Meaning

Athens

I saw
first from below
Athena's great ship
berthed on the Acropolis,
bright flags flying.

I touched
a fluted pillar,
gritty yet soft.
And I met Pericles,
the white sun shining.

I am your child, Athens,
the once-great city.
Your teachers taught me how to think.
Your polity is now my birthright;
Your golden fraction
enchants my eyes.

Approaching Venice from the Sea

Your spires spring forth
like fossil shards.
Your domes are the womb of heaven.
The blood of centuries
flows through your streets.

What would we know of love,
its tenderness and its safe haven,
if never we did lose a loved one,
or were betrayed by feckless lovers?

Were joy and gladness never ending,
Would we not be at risk for boredom?
Tears, sadness, despair, depression
help us plumb the depth of happiness.

If there were always light,
how would we know that it is so?
Knowledge that the sun alone gives life
comes to us in the dark of night.

Until death voids the difference
between dark and light.

Tomorrow is a womb
from which we're born anew.

Yesterday we died.
Today is all we'll ever know.

There is no order.
What we call order
is the fulfillment
of our expectations.

Just one event is certain,
my death and yours.
The rest is chance.

Words float at random
arrayed in patterns on the surface.
Meanings they seem to yield
seduce us readily into belief.

When they disaggregate
we do not know we are betrayed.
Misled by ineluctable formations,
we walk in truth until we fall.

Words can lead us into regions
where our pain resides.
Yet they can lift us into ecstasy,
and bring us healing love.

What would you see
if you could stand
outside yourself?

Would you know yourself
or see a stranger
looking back at you?

What if he spoke
and asked, "Who are you?"
How would you answer?

What if he turned
and walked away?
Would you ask him, "Why?"

Or, if you turned
the question on yourself,
how would you answer?

They are not truths about our lives,
the stories we have fashioned.
They are not truths about ourselves,
the tales we've learned to tell.
Most of us live in ignorance of
who we are
and witness our lives
as if in silvered shards.

We are alone,
every hour,
every day,
listening to thoughts
no one can hear.

Hiding behind our faces
not love,
but passion,
not anger
but rage,
and every thing
we greatly fear.

A rogue wave breaks—
When?
Was I there
to see its majesty?

A sky stretches
away from the horizon—
How far?
Did I see shadows?

Beyond the reach of space
where nowhere lies—
Have I been there?
And when?

Deep.
Deeper.
Is there a bottom?

I stand on ground.
I am this ground.

Must I pay a premium
for my life?
If so, then in what coin
and in whose realm?

Were I to give belief
to any one of many creeds,
I would be told its currency
and I would know its price;
but were I to forfeit its costly faith,
the price I paid for entry
would never be returned.

There is an answer to my question.
I must become the owner of my life.
I know the price I have to pay
in joy, in pain, in loss and in despair.
But in the end, I'd give myself away for love.

We trust each other no further
than that our freely given charity
is in time rewarded, if by nothing other
than self-respect.

We trust each other no further
than that unconditional love,
as we bear it to our children,
may move our progeny
to help us die in dignity.

We trust each other no further
than that we now possess the means
for our eternal self-destruction.

This moment,
intertwined with moments
lodged in memory,
enriches our understanding
of who we are and where.

And the moment that comes next
recollects times past
that change our apprehension
concerning who we are and where.

We sense a mystery
in how our lives were shaped
and of those who preceded us.
We hunger for its unraveling.

Perhaps in looking back,
in finding fossils and remains,
in teaching us their meaning,
that which is yet to come
will be revealed to us.

Pain is a flag
waving implacably,
unmoved by wind.

Pain is a place
without location.
It has no boundaries.

Pain is a time
without endurance.
It leaves no mark in memory.

To ease pain now
and in this moment
lift a passing mood.

Against all caution,
but pressed by urgencies
that others do not know,
at risk for fatal injury,
I drink the soothing wine
and am enraptured
by the smoke I breathe.

A fear commands me, entirely.
I am held fast in its dominion.
I am its prisoner for years.

Jackhammer obsessions
pound me without surcease,
break me into pointless fragments.

Lust holds me in its fist.
I cannot do other than I am bid,
until I am exploded.

I am at peace now,
but only in this moment.

Life is pain
and loss
and self-deprecation.

That's why many of us drink—
to numb the hurt,
to glow in triumph.

We pay a price,
and so do others,
for our way of life.

We cannot do otherwise.

Deep Depression

It is isolation in pain for which there are no words.
It is isolation in pain to which there is no end.
It is the paralysis of the will to live.
It is the wish to die.
It is the paralysis of the will to die.

I turn.
The window is barred.
I turn.
The door is locked.

My bed is a narrow pallet.
The floor is concrete.
A naked bulb hangs from the ceiling.
I am cold.

I fashioned this cell,
I locked myself in.

Hitler.
Few know and
fewer will agree
you were our teacher.

Hitler.
You taught us
we cannot kill
the hate we bear ourselves
by killing others.

Hitler.
You taught us
we are flawed
and that by Will alone
we cannot gain perfection.

Jesus, my friend,
our passion to destroy you
lay within our need
to bring you into life.

Because we die,
we are imperfect.
We did not know
that generations
would feed upon our lives.

We thought
that we were guilty
because we did not
love each other.

That's why we cast
ourselves from Paradise,
bent on our
guilty self-destruction.

You were the instrument
of our return.
We made you into love,
love always,
love everlasting.

And then we killed you.
We could not bear to look
into your eyes
and never see our own
in your reflection.

The day is not a bowl
into which your life is poured.
The day is a mosaic of moments.
Sometimes a pattern can be seen.
Sometimes it makes no sense.
All that is certain is that, at its borders,
it is light and it is dark.

As We Age

Aged.
Out of focus.

Forgetting
what has already been forgotten.

Captive to
irrelevant urgencies

It's not that death is near.
Pain is now.

I am betrayed
by time and its corrosion.
I have forgotten how to walk
and what my destination was.

I barely recognize
the person looking back at me.
I don't remember
why I'm shaving.

I used to read,
but when I do so now,
the words are indistinct,
and some have lost their meaning.

Age mates and I are outraged
by our betrayal and diminishment.
We share our misery,
but don't know who betrayed us.

Before us, in the end,
lies transformation or oblivion,
depending on our expectations.

Behind us, long ago,
lay love and loss,
not quite fulfilled ambitions,
triumphs and defeat.

We speak of nothing else.
We are old men.

Aging is a season of raging storms.
There is no shelter from the pain,
no refuge from infirmity.
You stumble through the muck.
The ground heaves up.
You have a fall.
You lose your dignity.
You may break bones
and forfeit life itself.

A fierce wind scatters all your memory.
Familiar words are blown away.
You can't remember how to tie your tie.
Appointments are forgotten.
The wind blows you into a rear-end smashup,
blurs your vision and your self-esteem.
Incurable illness, or fatal accident,
signals abatement of the storms.

For the most part, aging ends in indignity
and in intolerable pain.
Eased by medication into a final sleep,
we do not know the place in which we'll wake.
We do not know if such a place exists.

When You're in Your Eighties:

It's not about how many mistakes you make.
It's about how well and quickly you correct them.

It's not about how well you dress.
It's about how warm you are.

It's not about your interpersonal skills.
It's about having a social support group.

It's not about how many infirmities you have.
It's about having a skilled physical therapist.

It's not about how many children you have.
It's about how many of them have not inquired about your will.

It's not about how wealthy you may be.
It's about whether you can afford the medications.

It's not about still being able to drive.
It's about finding your car keys.

It's not about being free from pain.
It's about how well you can tolerate it.

It's not about being hospitalized.
It's about how well you can tolerate its discomforts.

In the end, it's not about how successfully you age.
It's about having someone who really loves you.

Facing Death

We cannot know
where she has gone.
We do know that we have lost
one of great value.

The death of a parent
is a milestone in our lives.
Our day is now quite empty
of what we knew as her unending presence.

Mothers are the origins of our lives.
Mostly for better, they are the mold
in which we form our own beginnings.
Lifelong, they are a token of who we have become.

We are alone now,
and responsible
for what we have yet to make
of our children and of ourselves.

Where from came death?
Why with its absolute authority
does it take from us
our awareness of who we are?

I do not recognize death's high authority.
I will not yield to its irrational command.
Being and knowing are my dear obsessions.
I choose not to surrender them.

Death is never the event
that leads us back to know our lives.

Death is an empty chalice
drained of meaning.

Death poses all those questions
that have no answer.

He who fashioned death
is not our friend.

He who fashioned death
is our enemy.

When towards the end,
the sum of life is negative.
You have outlived
those whom you valued highly.
Your children are in distant places
or in ambivalence.
Your body has become your enemy.
Dementia looms on a near horizon.

The imminence of death
may become a welcome prospect.

Reflections on a Childhood in Post–World War I Germany

Father,
I long for you.
Did you love me?
Did you ever love me?

In 1914 at Verdun,
your eyes were lost,
but you found me now,
and hurt me
with your large hands.

I killed you,
didn't I?
Why did I kill you?

I did not know why.
I do not know why.
Did I really kill you?
Did you love me,
Vaterchen?

The year is 1929.
I am in Berlin.
I am a child.

He roars in anger.
His sleep has been disturbed.
The blind man.

His arm is raised
to beat me.
The blind veteran.

He gropes for me.
I grab his hand.
The blind lieutenant.

He falls.
He loses consciousness.
The blind man.

Three months later,
he dies.
The blind man.

The year is 2010.
I no longer charge myself
with having killed my father,
the blind man.

I killed my brother
in cold blood.
He dared to claim my birthright.

I am the firstborn son.
My mother loves me only.
I claim all my father's pride.

I will not forgive my parents
for conceiving this usurper,
but I still claim their sole attention.

My name is Cain.
I bear the mark.
God has forbidden you to kill me.

Why?

My Aunt.
My mother's housekeeper.
She limped.
No, she waddled.
I thought it was the way older women walked.
Later they told me
she was deformed,
an invalid,
like others in my family.

I gave more care than I received.
I learned pity,
but not compassion.
Fear masked disgust,
and guilt protected against anger.

Now that she is dead,
what have I become?

Autobiography at Age Twelve

What can I not forget?
A kite.
I made it out of wrapping paper.

Cutting winds,
great clouds
at Helgoland,
far away.

Amber on the sand.
Splinters
in his feet
after he returned,
alone.
My brother.

The cobblestones we skated on
in winter,
in a lost city,
Berlin.

A blind man.
"I didn't wake you.
He did."

He sang
Lieder,
an alto tenor.

After three months, he died.
I don't know why.
It was a long walk to his grave
in Winter.

Christmas markets,
presents,
clay cast miniature German soldiers
and little tanks.

Always goose
and dumplings
with plums in them.

Mother,
always Mother.
A disciplining fabulist
given to long silences.
She had mastered the piano.
Beethoven still comforts me.
She died in 1962.

Ta Agnes,
my father's younger sister,
crippled from birth.
She died of malnutrition in 1944 in Berlin.

Tante Frieda,
my father's older sister.
She survived.

I was a sergeant in the US Army
of Occupation,
When I found her in the rubble
in Berlin
in September 1945.

And
Martin,
my beloved brother,
my feared and hated competitor.
He lost. I won.
Or was it the other way around?

Heil Hitler!
"Du bist ein verdammter Jude.
Rauss mit dir!"

Amerika:
Land of the banana split
And the ubiquitous soda.
America:
Land of unlimited possibilities.
The only place.